I0616146

The Anxiety Trap

Defeat Anxiety by the
Power of God
For Teens

Cindy Neubecker

**The Anxiety Trap © Copyright 2024 Cindy Neubecker
All rights reserved. This book or any portion thereof
may not be reproduced or used in any manner
whatsoever without the express written permission
of the publisher except for the use of brief quotations
in a book review.**

Scripture quotations marked TPT are from The Passion Translation®. Copyright © 2017, 2018, 2020 by Passion & Fire Ministries, Inc. Used by permission. All rights reserved. ThePassionTranslation.com.

Holy Bible, New Living Translation, Copyright © 1996, 2004, 2015 by Tyndale House Foundation. Used by permission of Tyndale House Publishers, Inc., Carol Stream, Illinois 60188. All rights reserved.

Scripture taken from the New King James Version®. Copyright © 1982 by Thomas Nelson. Used by permission. All rights reserved.

Scripture taken from the New Century Version®. Copyright © 2005 by Thomas Nelson. Used by permission. All rights reserved.

Scripture quotations marked (NIV) are taken from the Holy Bible, New International Version®, NIV®. Copyright © 1973, 1978, 1984, 2011 by Biblica, Inc.™ Used by permission of Zondervan. All rights reserved worldwide. www.zondervan.comThe "NIV" and "New International Version" are trademarks registered in the United States Patent and Trademark Office by Biblica, Inc.™

Scripture quotations marked (AMP) are taken from the Amplified Bible, Copyright © 2015 by The Lockman Foundation. Used by permission.

Scripture quotations marked (AMPCE) are taken from the Amplified Bible, Copyright © 1954, 1958, 1962, 1964, 1965, 1987 by The Lockman Foundation. Used by permission.

Dedication

This book is dedicated to my niece Kaylee, whose love for the Lord and desire to follow Him saved her from the anxiety trap.

Love you Kay!

Contents

Introduction

If you feel the torment of your thoughts spiraling into despair...

If you feel plagued with an anxious mind..

If you feel like there is no way out..

You're not alone in how you feel.
And you're in the anxiety trap.

I fell into the anxiety trap at a young age. My mind was tormented with thoughts of worry and despair running rampant. I tried everything I could to make it stop. All I wanted was to feel peace, but instead I felt like no one understood what I was going through and I was all alone.

But then something happened that changed everything and the next thing I knew I was free!

In this book I will tell you my story and how I escaped the trap. I've lived a long time out of the trap now and there are truly no adequate words to describe the feeling of freedom.

I remember how awful my life used to be. The crying, shaking and sweating for no reason. The tossing and turning at night as I worried about things that made very little sense.

I remember the constant feeling of dread as I waited expectantly for something bad to happen. Sometimes when the anxiety became too overwhelming, I would simply black out. It was a dark place to be and I am so glad I made it past that season in my life.

Because in the journey to healing I discovered the key to escaping the anxiety trap and that is what you'll find in this book. Read this book front to back, taking in every chapter with intense focus. Do what you learn within these pages and you will escape the anxiety trap just like I did.

This book is not meant to be a replacement for professional therapy. If you feel you need that, get it. This book is meant to equip you with God-given tools to defeat anxiety that would pair nicely with therapy or medicine if you feel like you need those.

If you are in the anxiety trap there is hope. It can change and it can get better. You do not have to live this way forever. I pray this book will help you as the contents of it helped me.

Psalm 25:15 (NLT) My eyes are always on the Lord, for he rescues me from the traps of my enemies.

My Story

As far back as I can remember, fear ruled my life. I felt like I was born afraid of everything. I was afraid I would die, afraid to go to school and afraid to talk to certain people. I had some scary things happen in my life, but the fear was there long before life threw some hard things my way.

Three people in my life died unexpectedly in the span of 4 years. My beloved grandfather died when I was 9. My cousin was hit by a car and died at 10 years old. I watched my aunt die of a heart attack when I was 13. Death seemed eerily close all the time.

My parents were loving and cared for me but were navigating many problems themselves. My father was an alcoholic, and although he was a pleasant one, he was drunk a lot. My mother was plagued with many types of sickness. And on top of that my younger brother was always in trouble with someone. We'd hear that he was in trouble with his teachers, the principal, other kids' parents, the police, you name it. So my home life had its challenges.

But I'm convinced that the fear and anxiety that ruled me would have been there regardless of my circumstances. It was there lurking inside long before there was any outside reason for it to exist.

No one has a perfect life and mine is no different. The anxiety inside me stayed there through the hard times. But when things were good I was no less fearful or anxious. It was just the way I was.

It was a regular occurrence for me to wake up crying for no reason. I was always nervous and worried about school or afraid I'd witness another person having a heart attack. I tried so hard to be perfect and was so afraid I'd never measure up to what I thought I should be.

My stomach was always in knots and death consumed my thoughts. I didn't want to end my own life, but I was afraid it was going to end early. Everything became a sign to me of my impending death. If I saw a light bulb go out, that meant my life was going out. If I heard someone on TV talk about death, I would think they were talking about me. As I think back to this now it sounds ridiculous. But at the time it was so real to me.

At school, when teachers would show a movie (on an old school projector) about staying away from drugs or not taking rides from strangers, there would always be a part of the movie that showed what could happen if you did those things. If they showed someone dying, I would faint. Right in class in front of everyone! It was so embarrassing. The fear and anxiety inside me overwhelmed me so much that my body couldn't take it and I would faint. It got so bad that if I walked into the classroom and just saw that projector I'd feel faint.

One time we read a book in class about someone dying, and I almost fainted right there. That time I was able to make myself calm down and I didn't faint thankfully. Apparently fainting was my way of escaping from profound fear and anxiety. My mother had to go in and tell my teachers about my problem and asked if they were going to show a movie or read anything about death to let me leave the room. I needed her to do that but it was so embarrassing for me as a teenager.

My doctor put me on medication for anxiety and since there weren't many resources to help kids like me at the time he had me come in each week and talk to him like a counseling session. One of these times, he taught me how my fear was causing a knot. It was a ball of tightened up muscle, which we could actually feel when we pressed on my stomach. I wanted to relax so much but I had such a hard time understanding how I would even do that. It felt hopeless.

I don't recall any benefit from the medicine at all, but I took it faithfully. Because of my regular fainting, my doctor ordered a bunch of tests to be done to see if they could find the problem. One they did was an EEG on my brain, where they attached wires to my head and watched my brain waves on a computer. They found no problem with my brain. They also did many blood tests all of which showed I was fine.

In the end they had no idea what was causing my anxiety and fainting so they told me that it might be hormones but they really weren't sure. My doctor was a nice man and tried so hard to get to the root of my problem, but he just couldn't. He recommended my mom take me to the pastor of our church. At that time we went to a church because the rest of our extended family went there. I don't remember learning anything much about the Bible or God. I'm not sure what they taught but whatever it was it didn't make much of an impact on me. My mom scheduled a visit with the pastor for her and I. It was a very uneventful meeting and didn't help me at all. I can't really remember much that was said but that meeting did however make my mom decide that we weren't going to that church anymore.

Around that time my mom heard a TV preacher teach about having a relationship with God and being born again. She gave her heart to the Lord right there in our living room. Shortly after that she told me all about what she had learned and about her growing relationship with the Lord. She told me I could pray and make Jesus Lord of my life too if I wanted. She made sure I knew it was my choice.

It seemed like the right thing to do to me so I gave my heart and life to the Lord in my bedroom one evening and asked him to lead my life. I really didn't know what I was doing to be honest but I remember the next day feeling so happy and content inside.

I told my friend on the bus about what I did and although I think she thought I was nuts, she was very nice and encouraging. But neither she nor I had any idea how much was starting to change inside me.

I'd love to tell you that all the anxiety I struggled with disappeared immediately. It didn't. But I was different inside. There was hope where there hadn't been before. The fear and anxiety still plagued me, but now for some reason I felt inside that there was a way out. The Holy Spirit must have been giving me hope, because I knew nothing about the Lord and his word at all.

My grandmother gave me my own Bible. It was a Living version and I could understand it. It didn't have all the "thee's and thou's" and strange words that other bibles did. It was written in a way that was easy for me to understand, but I had never liked reading. It was by far my least favorite thing to do. I had an awful time in school doing book reports because I disliked reading so much. My mom would often help me by reading the book to me so I could get the report done. But despite my hatred of reading, I just loved my Bible. I wanted to read it more than I had ever wanted to read any other book.

Over the next few years I developed a strong desire to know the Lord through his word. I read it and listened to people teach it all the time. I used my own money from babysitting to buy preaching tapes. (Yes, I'm talking about the little rectangular tapes that you put in a tape player. It was a long time ago.)

My family joined a church that taught the Bible and I got involved in a youth group. I learned so much over those years and loved every bit of it. I felt satisfied inside and I learned that I had more control over anxiety than I realized. I found out I could actually make it stop, and when I did I finally experienced the peace I so desperately wanted. I wasn't a slave to it anymore. It was a slave to me!

That trapped feeling left as I learned to control the source of anxiety and fear and I've never been the same since. It of course tries to come back sometimes and occasionally gets more of a foothold than it should. But I've learned how to get out of that trap every time. And now, I'm going to help you do the same thing.

In my story neither prescription drugs nor going to a pastor for counseling helped me escape the anxiety trap. But if those things are useful for you, then by all means take the help. Sometimes we need professional help to navigate through our own mind. However, what I am going to share with you will also help. So if you feel like you need it, get professional help and also implement what I'm going to teach you.

I finally conquered the anxiety and fear that was keeping me trapped when my heart was renewed and I gained some important knowledge that I had been missing.

I learned there is a real enemy named Satan who was plaguing me, but I had power over him. That may sound scary but don't let it scare you. There is nothing to be afraid of, just a battle to win and a trap to get out of, and you can do both.

I know what it's like to have an anxious, fearful heart and not know why you feel the way you do.

I know what it's like to wake up crying in the middle of the night, raked with fear and not know how to make it stop.

I know what it's like to have a problem that no one around you knows how to solve.

It's a lonely place and I know it well but I also found the way out. I have found the door and I want to lead you to that door, dear reader.

If you are tired of anxiety and fear attacking your mind day and night and living in a constant spiral of misery, you have finally found the answer you've been looking for. In just a short time you will feel so differently. The thoughts that plague you now will have no power over you. If they try to sneak back into your mind, you will quickly toss them out because you will know what it's like to live in peace, and that's the way you'll want to live all the time.

According to the Oxford Languages Dictionary, the definition of anxiety is a feeling of worry, nervousness or unease, typically about an imminent event or something with an uncertain outcome. Anxiety is real and it's wrapped in fear. They go hand in hand.

Be aware of using anxiety as a status symbol and telling all your friends about it. That is a dangerous game to play with your own mind. It may seem cool to have an anxiety and fear problem and it will get you some attention, but it's not worth lying about. Your words are very important and what you say (especially about yourself) carries a lot of weight. We will talk more about this later. Just know that pretending to have anxiety is not cool because it will create an actual anxiety problem inside you.

Nobody who has ever had real anxiety wants to be in the clutches of it. It's a horrible trap and a miserable place for your mind to be. It affects your whole being. Your heart beats faster than it should, your breathing gets shallow, and it gets hard to eat and sleep. Your thoughts are filled with fear and it becomes hard for you to be the person you were created to be.

But you can escape this trap for good and never fall back into it.

Let me show you how.

Jesus Loves Me, This I Know

Have you ever heard the song Jesus Loves Me?

"Jesus loves me this I know
For the Bible tells me so.
Little ones to him belong.
They are weak, but he is strong.
Yes Jesus loves me,
Yes Jesus loves me,
Yes Jesus loves me,
The Bible tells me so".

If you don't know the song, Google it and listen to the tune. It's a cute song and the words are true. Unfortunately many people have no idea what true love is. That might be true for you. If it is, this type of song means nothing. And for me to tell you "God loves you" doesn't mean anything. It may even bring on painful thoughts for you.

If your earthly father has no idea how to love you, or maybe he has been abusive, manipulative, or simply ignored your existence, the idea of a loving heavenly father God may be a very strange thing to you. You may have been loved by your parents but taught incorrectly that God is just waiting for you to mess up so he can punish you.

Maybe you thought acting perfectly was the only way to be loved by God and you know you've done some things you shouldn't have, so God must not love you. Maybe love was used as a weapon, and if you weren't good it was withheld. Or maybe you have great parents who love you, but you've never experienced God's love, so it's hard to imagine.

Let me tell you God's love is not like anything else. There's nothing that can compare. He doesn't use his love against you. It's not a weapon. It's pure, sweet, comforting and strong. It's impossible to totally describe how wonderful it is. One of the best ways to describe it is in the Bible verse

I Corinthians 13:4-8a (TPT) Love is large and incredibly patient. Love is gentle and consistently kind to all. It refuses to be jealous when blessing comes to someone else. Love does not brag about one's achievements nor inflate its own importance. Love does not traffic in shame and disrespect, nor selfishly seek its own honor. Love is not easily irritated or quick to take offense. Love joyfully celebrates honesty and finds no delight in what is wrong. Love is a safe place of shelter, for it never stops believing the best for others. Love never takes failure as defeat, for it never gives up. Love never stops loving.

That is how God loves you. Isn't that amazing? Incidentally that is also how he wants us to love others but we will talk about that later.

When you have someone you really love you think about them all the time don't you? Well God thinks about you all the time too. It says in the Bible in **Psalms 139:17-18 (NLT) How precious are your thoughts about me, O God. They cannot be numbered! I can't even count them; they outnumber the grains of sand! And when I wake up, you are still with me!**

That is hard to imagine for us humans isn't it? But this isn't hard for the God who created the universe. And he doesn't have to love us at all. I mean let's face it, we all act like jerks sometimes and do and say things we shouldn't. But God loves us anyway.

God thinks about you all the time too.

Did you know that God loves you so much he is concerned with every part of your being? He knows everything about you - even how many hairs are on your head at any time. The average amount of hairs on a human head is about 100,000. We lose between 50-100 a day and we grow 50-100 a day. Considering there are approximately 8.1 billion people on the earth right now that's a lot of math just to track your hair. Only someone who truly loves you would do that. But look at this!

Matthew 10:29-31 (NLT) What is the price of two sparrows - one copper coin? But not a single sparrow can fall to the ground without your Father knowing it. And the very hairs on your head are all numbered. So don't be afraid; you are more valuable to God than a whole flock of sparrows.

God has proved to us he loved us in so many ways. He's created us and the world we live in with the flowers, mountains, rivers, oceans, fish, animals as well as your cute dog, cat or hamster. In fact, every good thing that's been created came from God. He either did it himself or worked through people by showing them what to do. All the great things you enjoy came from God. His Word, and from this point on that's what we will call the Bible, says in **James 1:17 (NLT) Whatever is good and perfect is a gift coming down to us from God our Father, who created all the lights in the heavens.**

He created all these things because he loves us. We could be walking around on a blah looking gray earth with no color and no fun things to enjoy. But God loves us too much to not give us the best stuff. In fact the biggest way he proved he loves us was by sending his son Jesus to die on the cross for us. This may seem like an odd thing to do but I'll explain.

Adam and Eve were the first people God created. He told them they could eat any food in the lovely garden of Eden where they lived. But he told them not to eat from the tree in the center of the garden called the Tree of the Knowledge of Good and Evil.

The devil came and tricked Eve into eating the fruit of that tree (which was not necessarily an apple as many think, The Word only calls it fruit not an apple). Adam ate it also. What they did by disobeying God is called sin. Sin is defined as missing the mark. In other words they shouldn't have done it. And because they were the first people, and they sinned, they brought sin into the world.

By obeying the devil instead of God they gave him more power and ability to do his dirty work. Everyone born after them sinned because sin was now in the human race. Right down to you and me and everyone coming after us. Sin is in the world now and everyone sins. It doesn't matter how good you think someone is, they sin in some way. No one is perfect and it's because we can't be.

But God is holy and perfect and cannot look at sin. So he came up with a way to take sin away so that he could look at his people again. The way he devised to take sin away was by blood. So people would sacrifice a lamb or another animal every year and the blood of that animal covered the sins they did that year. They would be forgiven for all their sins that year, and year after year they would sacrifice another animal to take care of their sins again. It must have been a messy and gory thing to have to do every year. I know it sounds gross and I agree. But that is how God made it.

Then God made a better way to accomplish getting rid of sin because He loves us. He sent Jesus, his son, to be born on earth through a woman named Mary. Stay with me here as this can sound weird but once you get this so deep down in your heart you will never be the same.

You see Jesus was a part of God, and God placed him in Mary, so he could be part God and part human. He lived a perfect life, then died on the cross as our sacrifice for all time. He is called the perfect lamb of God because when he died, his blood was shed and he took all our sins on himself. He paid for our sin forever. We never have to sacrifice an animal to cover our sin again. Jesus took care of it. He carried our sin, sickness, poverty and pain on himself for us. God could not even look at him on the cross because of that sin which he didn't commit but carried for you and me.

If you've ever seen a plaque or piece of jewelry with Jesus hanging on a cross, they look so pleasant. But it was not pleasant. It was an awful site. Actually the Word says in **Isaiah 52:14 (NCV) Many people were shocked when they saw him. His appearance was so damaged he did not look like a man; his form was so changed they could barely tell he was human.**

Did you read that? He didn't even look like a human because he was so mangled. Sin and its consequences are very ugly.

Yet he was willing to do that for you and me because he loves us so much. All you have to do is believe it and choose to let him be your Lord, the one who directs your life. Let me tell you it's the best deal you'll ever take because I'm certain I'd mess up my life completely if I didn't let him lead the way. Since he created us, loves us, and shed his blood for us, it only makes sense to let him be our Lord and lead us.

Think about it, God was willing to send his son whom he loves so much to go through the worst possible thing a person could go through so that he could be in a relationship with you and

> **It only makes sense to let him be our Lord and lead us.**

me. Being disconnected from us was something he couldn't bear because he loves us so much. How amazing! Jesus willingly did it because he loves us and he did this knowing that you may never believe in him or make him your Lord. Yet he made sure you had that option.

God, Jesus and the Holy Spirit are one person in three parts. If you choose to believe in what Jesus did for you, the Holy Spirit will come and live in your heart to help you follow the Lord. You cannot see him, but he's there helping you think and do the right things. And he so deeply loves you. You can completely ignore him and give him no attention if you want to, never listening to him at all, and he knows that is possible.

Yet he is still willing to be there for you any time if you will listen and he can help. That is love. Here are a few verses the Word gives us about this.

John 3:16 (NLT) **"For this is how God loved the world: He gave his one and only Son, so that everyone who believes in him will not perish but have eternal life.**

I John 4:10 **(NLT)** **This is real love—not that we loved God, but that he loved us and sent his Son as a sacrifice to take away our sins.**

Romans 5:8 **(NLT) But God showed his great love for us by sending Christ to die for us while we were still sinners.**

If you are ready to pray and ask Jesus to be Lord of your life and have the Holy Spirit come live in your heart, we have a prayer written out in the back of this book that you can pray called the Salvation Prayer. Just read it out loud to the Lord and he will hear you. You need to mean it in your heart and be for real. This is what becoming a Christian is all about. This is how its done. It's not a bunch of do's and don'ts. It's receiving what Jesus did for you and living for him.

I always advise people that after they pray a salvation prayer to tell someone. It would help to tell another Christian if you know one and they will celebrate hugely with you! This is the best decision you've ever made in your life. And it's required to escape the anxiety trap.

Trust the Love

Once we've found out how much God loves us our next step after committing our lives to him is to trust the love. The devil would like you to think that God loves everybody but you, but don't listen to him. He's a liar.

I John 4:16 (NLT) We know how much God loves us, and we have put our trust in his love. God is love, and all who live in love live in God, and God lives in them.

It's impossible to rely on love you don't trust. Trust may be a hard thing for you if the people around you always let you down. But you can learn to trust God. People aren't perfect, but God is and he doesn't lie or change.

If you've had bad things happen to you it doesn't mean God doesn't love you. It means the devil wants to mess up your life. We haven't talked much about him, but he is real and doesn't like anyone God loves, which is all of us.

The Word says in **John 10:10 (AMPCE) The thief comes only in order to steal and kill and destroy. I came that they may have and enjoy life, and have it in abundance (to the full, till it overflows).**

The thief this verse is talking about here is the devil. The one speaking or the "I" in this verse is Jesus. He came to give us a good life. So when the devil or your own mind tries to convince you that God doesn't love you, don't believe it. Choose to trust the love God has for you even when you don't feel a thing.

Because God loves you, he's always there for you. You can talk to him about anything and everything and should talk to him regularly. That is called prayer. It's not formal and you don't have to be on your knees with you eyes closed or in a church but you can if you want. Anywhere you are is the right place to talk to the Lord. He hears you and wants to help you in every situation. I talk to him about pretty much everything, even small things that don't seem important, like where I should park my car at the store or if I should text a particular person right now.

He wants to lead us and help us with everything. Nothing is too small or too big to talk to God about. He loves us so much He cares about everything we do or think or feel.

If we follow what we feel He's leading us to do, our days are much better. Remember, though, that God is a gentleman. He won't barge into your day without access from you. If you ask, then you've given him access and he will gladly help.

Prayer is the way to make and keep a strong relationship with the Lord. Just like you need to talk to your friends or family regularly or your relationship starts to fall apart, so we need to communicate with our father God.

Talk to God

As you probably know, communication is a two-way thing. We can't just talk to our friends and have them never respond and call that a relationship can we? Well God responds to us. He communicates with us in a few different ways.

- He talks to us through his Word (the Bible). He will lead you to scripture that will answer your questions and lead you in your decisions.

- The Holy Spirit who comes to live inside us when we make Jesus our Lord is always speaking to our conscious. Sometimes you'll just know what to do and you'll feel good and peaceful about it, that is the Holy Spirit leading.

- Other people can also be the voice of God to you. They may not even know he's using them but they will say something that you just know was the Lord speaking to you.

- Circumstances (sometimes) can be the Lord's way of speaking or leading us. But we must be careful about always being led that way because the devil can also mess with our circumstances and we don't want to follow him. You can always ask for confirmation from God to make sure you are going the right way or doing the right thing. He will be happy to let you know if you are on the right track by one of the other ways he speaks.

God leads us with peace, not anxiety. He never manipulates us or makes us feel guilty or fearful. Even if he speaks correction to us, it has love and peace attached to it. Sometimes we need to be corrected and when we do he'll let us know. He corrects us by his Holy Spirit within us. You will just know inside that you've done something wrong. Or he corrects us with his Word. You will read something and have a tug on your heart that there is something you need to change.

Sometimes he corrects us by using another person to point something out we missed. When you feel he's correcting something you've done, just repent, which means to tell him you are sorry and change the behavior. God will even help you to do what's right when you ask him.

The most important thing is that we believe the love God has for us and don't ever forget that, no matter what happens in your life.

If something bad happens, don't automatically think it is because God doesn't love you or is angry with you or let you down. There can be many causes for bad things to happen. It could be that the devil managed to get what he wanted, people made bad decisions, or mistakes were made by someone that has affected you etc… It is never because God doesn't love you. No matter what happened in the past, you can trust his love for you. He is with you and will help you through whatever comes along.

Are you having trouble believing God loves you? Then do this; Ask God to show you that he loves you somehow. You may even be having a hard time believing God is even real.

If something bad happens, don't automatically think it is because God doesn't love you.

Then ask him if he's real to show you he loves you. He will do it. It may take a little time or may be right away, but he will show you he loves you. When he does you will know it. God loves you more than anyone else ever has or ever will.

Eat Up

Pizza, I love it. It's my favorite food. I love it with just about any toppings (except anchovies) and lots of sauce and cheese. I could eat it everyday and probably wouldn't get sick of it although I've never tested that theory. Of course I eat healthy foods also. I know my body needs all the vitamins, minerals, protein and other things to keep it healthy. You probably know that too whether you like it or not. Feeding our bodies takes time, thought and planning. We do that because we know how important it is and we enjoy it, I mean who doesn't enjoy eating?

But did you know that there are other parts of you that also need to be fed besides your stomach? Actually there are three different parts of you that need to be fed. You are a spirit, you have a soul and you live in a body.

Body

You obviously know that you have a body and you know that you have to feed it. But let me tell you some things maybe you didn't know about your body. In order to live and function on the earth we need a physical body. We get this body by being formed in our mother's womb and being born. At the moment our body begins to form at conception, we are given a spirit and soul that live within our bodies.

Our spirit and soul is who we are and our body is our earth suit. It gives us the right and ability to live on earth. This is why Jesus was born of a woman, to get an earth suit. Our spirit and soul will live eternally and can live without our body but our body dies when our spirit and soul leave it. So you see our body isn't just a body it houses our spirit and soul. So now let's look at our soul.

Soul

Our soul is defined as our mind, will and emotions. It's our personality. Neither our soul or spirit can be seen by our eyes but that does not mean they aren't both very real. We know they are different because the Word says in **Hebrews 4:12 (NLT) For the word of God is alive and powerful. It is sharper than the sharpest two-edged sword, cutting between soul and spirit, between joint and marrow. It exposes our innermost thoughts and desires.** This verse says a few different things but the point we want to bring out here is that it says that the soul and spirit are two different things that can be separated.

As with our bodies, our souls need to be fed. And as with our bodies vitamins, minerals etc. our souls have certain things they need. We all need to socialize with people. We need friends and family to connect with. It's very important to the health of your soul to spend time with other people talking and having fun.

You don't have to have a ton of friends or relatives but if you have a few people you can spend time with now and then in person not just with texts or Facetime but in each other's presence, that's very good for your soul. Beyond that, feeding your soul becomes more personal. If you like reading, taking walks, cooking, drawing, playing piano or guitar or whatever, doing those things will feed your soul. Fun and healthy things feed your soul. God made you a particular way to like certain things and those things are good for you to do.

Be careful with too much social media as a way to feed your soul. It actually can do the opposite and hurt your soul but we will talk more about that in a later chapter. So you be you and don't gauge what you like by what other people like. Find what fills your soul and do that as often as you when you can. It's good for you.

Spirit

Your spirit is the invisible real you. It's not a ghost nor will you ever be a ghost when you die. That is a man-made idea and is not true. You will never get to come back and haunt anyone. That is not how it works.

Your spirit looks just like you and has your face and your height. If anyone who knows you now saw your spirit, they would know it was you. Here is a scripture that shows this.

Matthew 17:1-3 (NLT) Six days later Jesus took Peter and the two brothers, James and John, and led them up a high mountain to be alone. 2 As the men watched, Jesus' appearance was transformed so that his face shone like the sun, and his clothes became as white as light. 3 Suddenly, Moses and Elijah appeared and began talking with Jesus.

Moses and Elijah had died many years before the time this verse is talking yet Jesus saw them and was talking to them. He was talking to their spirits. They didn't have physical bodies anymore. But they looked just like they had when they lived on this earth and had bodies. This may seem a bit deep. Don't get too caught up in this, just know you are a spirit.

Your spirit is eternal, meaning it will live forever. We know this because when you die your body is dead but your spirit goes to either heaven or hell. We discussed making Jesus your Lord and that is what determines whether your spirit ends up in heaven or hell, not how good you've been. If Jesus is your Lord and you are what we call "saved" then you have received God's forgiveness of your sins and your spirit will be in heaven. You don't have to wonder about that.

We feed our spirits only one way, with spirit food which is the Word of God. **John 6:63b (NKJV) The words that I speak to you are spirit, and they are life.**

God's word is itself spirit food. When we don't feed our spirit, it becomes unhealthy. If we could see most people's spirit, we would see a puny skinny little thing that is unbalanced and unhealthy. It's our spirits that communicate with God by way of the Holy Spirit. To have a healthy balanced spirit that can hear God, I recommend reading or listening to the word every day. Just like you eat physical food every day. One meal of food a week won't keep our bodies strong and healthy and one meal of the word a week won't keep our spirits strong and healthy either.

Matthew 4:4(NKJV) But He answered and said, "It is written, 'Man shall not live by bread alone, but by every word that proceeds from the mouth of God.' "

Just like physical food gives us nutrients and strength to do what we do, God's word does the same thing for us.

II Timothy 3:16 (NLT) All Scripture is inspired by God and is useful to teach us what is true and to make us realize what is wrong in our lives. It corrects us when we are wrong and teaches us to do what is right.

You may wonder why I mentioned in my own story that reading the Bible got rid of my anxiety. Isn't it only a book after all? Good question. The Bible isn't like any other book. It isn't just a book of stories about people who lived long ago like a history book. It's alive. Alive you ask? Yes, alive.

We referenced this verse already but let's look at it again.

Hebrews 4:12 (NLT) For the word of God is alive and powerful. It is sharper than the sharpest two-edged sword, cutting between soul and spirit, between joint and marrow. It exposes our innermost thoughts and desires.

Let's also look at the same verse in a different version of the Bible.

Hebrews 4:12 (TPT) For we have the living Word of God, which is full of energy, like a two-mouthed sword. It will even penetrate to the very core of our being where soul and spirit, bone and marrow meet! It interprets and reveals the true thoughts and secret motives of our hearts.

This verse clearly says that the Bible is a living book. I know that is hard to understand but it's true. Bill Johnson, the pastor at Bethel church in Redding, Ca. says "the Bible is the only book where when you read it the author shows up." That is such a great statement. If you have made Jesus Lord of your life then the Holy Spirit lives in your heart. When you read the Bible, he is right there to help you understand it and do what it says. He knows what you need, and if you let him lead you to where you need to read, it will help you grow spiritually healthy and know the Lord better. And being spiritually healthy means you can get out of the anxiety trap.

Another way to feed your spirit is hearing teaching about the word of God. There are lots of great podcasts made by some really good Bible teachers that can help you understand God's word. I listen to some that help me continue to grow and know God better. I also make teaching podcasts to teach what I know to others. Of course going to a good Bible believing church is a good place to learn, and getting involved in Bible studies with people around your age is also helpful and fun.

Seek to know God through his word in whatever ways work best for you. We never stop growing in our knowledge of the Lord. And that means we will never get bored in our Christian life. We will be forever learning about God and knowing him better than we did the day before. We will never be able to say we know it all because that will not happen. He is too big and too complex to ever be fully understood by us. But we still can have the most wonderful relationship with him as we seek to know him better.

The better you know the Lord the more you realize how good he is and how much he wants to help you get rid of the anxiety and be free. He didn't create you to be full of fear. When I began feeding my spirit the word of God, that, along with the love of God, drove that nasty heavy fear and anxiety out of my heart. It would rear its ugly head sometimes and try to come back on me and still does now sometimes.

But staying consistent in the word of God and believing what it says gets rid of it each time. If I can do it, so can you!

God is not the author of fear, the devil is, and yes he is real. He would like to control your life with fear so you never get on the path God has for you. Fear-based decisions, which are decisions made in fear, will lead you in the wrong direction with your life. The devil likes to keep you miserable with a constant nagging feeling of impending doom. But he's a liar. God has a wonderful life planned for you and he is so excited to walk with you through it.

Getting to know God in his word will help you discover that there is much to look forward to and nothing to be afraid of or anxious about. Also in God's word you will discover how much power and authority you have over the devil.

God is not the author of fear, the devil is.

He is nothing to be afraid of at all, you are much more powerful than he is. He's nothing compared to you.

Authority Over the Enemy

Authority: The legal power or right to command or act, power to give orders or make decisions.

We are all under someone else's authority. You may be under your parents authority because of your age and you live in their home. If you have a job, your boss has authority over you. Teachers, professors, older relatives, police, and others have authority over your life in some way. They can give orders and make decisions that you have to obey. But you also have authority. God gave it to you to use. No matter how old you are or what you've ever done, you have authority if Jesus is your Lord.

Who do you have authority over?

Luke 10:19 (NLT) Look, I have given you authority over all the power of the enemy, and you can walk among snakes and scorpions and crush them. Nothing will injure you.

The enemy in this verse is the devil. Snakes and scorpions refers to the sly cunning ways of the devil and his sting. So what does that even mean? It means you have the right to stop his attacks on you. In the Bible it tells us clearly that God did not and will not give us anxiety and fear.

II Timothy 1:7 (AMP) For God did not give us a spirit of timidity or cowardice or fear, but [He has given us a spirit] of power and of love and of sound judgment and personal discipline [abilities that result in a calm, well-balanced mind and self-control].

Anxiety is caused by fear and did not come from God.

The kind of fear that causes anxiety and messes with our ability to enjoy life is from the devil. We can stop him from dumping that kind of fear on us. But if you don't know that you have that kind of authority, you won't use it and the devil will then attack you with fear as much as he wants. His goal is always to kill, steal, and destroy.

John 10:10 (NLT) The thief's purpose is to steal and kill and destroy. My purpose is to give them a rich and satisfying life.

This verse was spoken by Jesus when he was on the earth. He is clearly saying that the devil does bad things and he does good. Remember this point. It will help you in the future. The devil is bad and God is good. It's a simple concept but you'd be surprised how people mix that up and blame God for the bad things that happen. God wants us to have a good life and the enemy wants us to be miserable. He will kill, steal, and destroy your relationships, your self esteem, your joy, and your very life if he can.

But you don't have to let him. You can stop him. And by the way just because you can't see him doesn't mean he isn't real. He is as real as you are and Jesus is also just as real as anything that can be seen. Don't judge what is real by what you see.

Don't let yourself get deceived into thinking the devil is not real. If you do, he'll be able to get away with a lot of destruction in your life. He is hoping you will always think he's not the one who did those bad things. It's a sneaky trick he uses to deceive people. He makes them think he's not real. He can and does get away with a lot that way because no one addresses what they think isn't real.

How do you use your authority?

To be able to use your authority, you have to first understand the name of Jesus. Why does his name matter? Well his name matters very much because we use that name to defeat the devil. Let's look at a couple scriptures that tell us about Jesus' name.

Philippians 2:9-11 (TPT) Because of that obedience, God exalted him and multiplied his greatness! He has now been given the greatest of all names! 10 The authority of the name of Jesus causes every knee to bow in reverence! Everything and everyone will one day submit to this name—in the heavenly realm, in the earthly realm, and in the demonic realm. 11 And every tongue will proclaim in every language: "Jesus Christ is Lord Yahweh," bringing glory and honor to God, his Father!

Luke 10:17 (NLT) When the seventy-two disciples returned, they joyfully reported to him, "Lord, even the demons obey us when we use your name!"

You can see from these verses that the name of Jesus is very important and powerful. It is not a name to be thrown around or used to swear or cuss. We talked about how to make Jesus Lord of your life. That process can also be referred to as being born again, being saved, becoming a Christ follower or becoming a Christian. Whatever you want to call it, it requires you to call on the name of Jesus.

Romans 10:13 (NLT) For "Everyone who calls on the name of the Lord will be saved."

Call on here means to call Jesus by his name and speak to him. God gave us the name of Jesus to accomplish certain things. We are told to pray in Jesus' name also.

John 23:24 (NIV) In that day you will no longer ask me anything. Very truly I tell you, my Father will give you whatever you ask in my name. Until now you have not asked for anything in my name. Ask and you will receive, and your joy will be complete.

To come to God in Jesus name means we have the right as imperfect people to come before a perfect God because Jesus took our sin and made us perfect in God's eyes. He sees us through what Jesus did for us.

Jesus Name and Your Words

You can start your prayer in Jesus name or end it in Jesus name or both. I usually do both. I start my prayer like this "Father I come to you in Jesus name." Then I talk to him about whatever is on my mind. Then I end my prayer with "in Jesus name." The reason to pray this way is because the Lord told us to in his word. If you totally don't understand why, just do it because he said so and someday it will make sense if it doesn't now.

Now keep the importance of Jesus' name in your thinking as we move on to learning about the power of the words you choose to speak. I'll connect these two things together later to explain how to use your authority against the devil and his anxiety trap.

Sticks and stones may break my bones but words will never hurt me. Have you ever heard that saying? Well it's not true. Words can hurt much worse than a broken bone and the effects can last long after that bone is healed. God has given us our own free will and with that we have the right to choose the words we speak. Our words can help or hurt ourselves as well as others. What we speak profoundly affects the world around us. This is a very deep subject but I'm not going to go too deep with it here. Just know that our words are very important. They don't just go out and dissolve in the air.

They don't just go out and dissolve in the air. They are powerful and can cause things to happen that you may or may not like. You can't even get saved without speaking.

Romans 10:9-10 (NIV) If you declare with your mouth, "Jesus is Lord," and believe in your heart that God raised him from the dead, you will be saved. 10 For it is with your heart that you believe and are justified, and it is with your mouth that you profess your faith and are saved.

The devil can hear your words. He listens to what we say. He also has to do what he's told when we use Jesus' name. God is bigger than the devil and much much more powerful. God lives in you if Jesus is your Lord.

I John 4:4 (NIV) You, dear children, are from God and have overcome them, because the one who is in you is greater than the one who is in the world.

The "one who is in the world" that this verse is talking about is the devil. And he has to submit to the name of Jesus.

Philippians 2:9-11 (NIV) Therefore God exalted him to the highest place and gave him the name that is above every name, that at the name of Jesus every knee should bow, in heaven and on earth and under the earth, and every tongue acknowledge that Jesus Christ is Lord, to the glory of God the Father.

Notice that every being will bow, meaning to give honor to the name of Jesus. That means Satan has to also. So to use your authority over the devil you have to speak and command him in Jesus name. You do that by speaking your God-given rights. Jesus paid for your sin so you have no need to carry guilt over it.

I Peter 2:24 (NIV) "He himself bore our sins" in his body on the cross, so that we might die to sins and live for righteousness; "by his wounds you have been healed."

He wants to give us a good life.

John 10:10 (NIV) The thief comes only to steal and kill and destroy; I have come that they may have life, and have it to the full.

These are just a few of the promises that God made to us in his word.

Anything God promised to you in his word is yours and you have the right to have it. But you will probably have to fight with the devil to get it cause he's a thief and he will steal anything he can. So when he comes to give us anxiety and steal from us our peace of mind which is promised to us we have the right and authority to drive him out. We've looked at it before but let's look at it again in a different version.

Luke 10:19 (TPT) Now you understand that I have imparted to you my authority to trample over his kingdom. You will trample upon every demon before you and overcome every power Satan possesses.

Don't you love that? I sure do. We aren't sitting ducks waiting to be attacked. We can do something about it. You have authority over all the power of the enemy. And you use that authority by speaking what God's word promises and telling him to flee in Jesus name.

Say you are feeling fine and something happens and all the sudden your stomach tightens up and you feel sweaty and shaky and your heart starts racing, an anxiety attack is coming on. An attack is exactly what is happening. The devil is attacking you. You fight back by saying out loud "You spirit of fear, I drive you out of my life right now in the name of Jesus"! You don't have to use those exact words but make sure you're using the name of Jesus. The spirit of fear is one of the devil's tools he uses to attack us and it is a spirit.

II Timothy 1:7 (NLT) For God has not given us a spirit of fear and timidity, but of power, love, and self-discipline.

The Bible tells us that when we resist the devil he will flee from us.

James 4:7 (NLT) So humble yourselves before God. Resist the devil, and he will flee from you.

Resist means to withstand, oppose, to set against. What this means is we don't sit back and take it. We don't say "well this is just me I have anxiety." We stand against it. Tell the fear to shut up! Don't entertain the fear-filled thoughts in your mind. Don't take anxiety as something you just have to live with, because you don't!

I thought I'd be anxious and fearful my whole life. Then I found out that wasn't true. If I put up with it, I'd keep it. If I would stand against it in Jesus' name, it would go away. This doesn't mean it will stay gone. You will probably have to use your authority against it many times and for a while. He will leave each time but often comes right back. The devil is tenacious and will keep trying to wear you down. He will keep pushing but if you keep pushing back you will win. I can tell you this because I won. But that is not to say I haven't had to stand against him again a number of times in my life, because I have. But it's not a long fight and I can deal with it quickly. He doesn't attack with fear and anxiety very often anymore.

I am a completely different person than I was as a young girl. When I tell people that I had an anxiety problem when I was young most of them have a hard time believing it.

This will be the same way for you when you overcome the anxiety trap for good. People won't even believe you ever struggled with it.

One more thing I want you to understand about your authority in Christ is what you have authority over and what you don't.

You do have authority over the devil and his demons. The Bible promises you that. You do have authority over yourself what you do and what you think about and what you say. You can control those things. Many people think they can't control their own thoughts, but they can. You have the ability to think what you want to think. Practice it. When a fear filled thought comes into your mind, drive out the devil first in case he's the one whispering those thoughts to you. Then if you still keep thinking fearful things, make yourself stop and think about things that make you happy. You can do it. In fact the Bible tells us to do it.

Philippians 4:8 (NLT) And now, dear brothers and sisters, one final thing. Fix your thoughts on what is true, and honorable, and right, and pure, and lovely, and admirable. Think about things that are excellent and worthy of praise.

If we could not control what we think the Bible would not tell us to do that. The Holy Spirit will help you do this and you should practice it often.

What you do not have authority over is another person's will. God gave us all a free will and he will not take that away from us. Free will means we have the right to make our own decisions. God himself will not make you do anything. He will give you ideas and ability and reasons to do certain things and the Holy Spirit will try to make you see what you should do. But the final decision is still yours, always.

For instance the Bible says God wants everyone to make Jesus their Lord but not everyone does, because it's their choice. You have authority over yourself and when you have children you will have authority over them until they become adults. Then they will have their own will and authority. So use the authority God has given you correctly and you'll start to get out of the anxiety trap.

42

Don't Open the Door

To keep our minds free from anxiety, it's important to not let things into our minds that cause fear. Fear is the cause of anxiety.

When you let your mind drift to thinking about all the bad things that could happen and those miserable "what ifs," you fall more easily into anxiety.

I used to constantly think, "what if I fail? What if people don't like me? What if I'm alone? What if I can't get the job I want? What if? What if? what if?"

Those kinds of thoughts set us up for an anxious mind. Then we are trapped in our anxiety.

The best thing to do is stop that before it starts. Do yourself a favor. Don't set yourself up for that kind of thinking. Avoid the things that stir that up. Things such as scary movies and shows, scary books, even video games that are really graphic with killing and mutilation or anything that promotes fear. Don't play with fear. It doesn't play nice. And you have the ability to control what comes into your mind.

Did you know that your eyes and ears are doors? They are doors to your soul and you have the key to those doors. What you allow in those doors is what will be inside you.

You let things inside by what you watch, look at or listen to. If you let scary, fearful, sad, and violent things in the doors of your eyes and ears, it's very hard to get them out. And those things feed anxiety. If you want to be free from fear, don't open the door to it. You may think "I can handle it. I've watched these things tons of times and it's never been a problem." Are you experiencing anxiety? Then it's been a problem and you didn't know what was feeding it. The truth is every single person is negatively affected if they choose to watch something scary. A little fear let into us is like taking a little poison. It may not kill you but it can sure make you feel bad.

As a kid I used to love to watch scary movies on Saturday T.V. I loved the thrill of the scare. I'd hide my face in a pillow when the worst parts would be on the screen. When the show was over I remember having the most yucky feeling inside. I always figured it would just go away. But it didn't for many years. I don't think the anxiety started with these shows but they certainly aggravated the situation. I had created a playground for the devil in my head by opening the doors of my eyes and ears to those things.

When I was learning these things myself and was making progress in getting out of the anxiety trap as a teenager my cousins, whom I loved and wanted to impress, came to visit one day.

They suggested we go see the newest scary movie that had just come out. They were older than me and I didn't want to look like a scared little baby, so I went with them to the movie. Inside myself I really knew it wasn't a good idea since I was finally getting over all the fear and anxiety I had been dealing with but I went anyway. It was a very scary movie and I was almost sick to my stomach when we came out of the theater. In the parking lot I made the announcement to my cousins that I would never go see a movie like that again. They didn't think I was weird. They actually agreed.

That set me back with my anxiety issues. It all started to come back. I realized that the Holy Spirit inside me was trying to tell me not to go and I didn't listen and went anyway. That was a wrong choice. I needed to repent to the Lord for being disobedient. Repent means to admit what you did was wrong, ask for forgiveness and not to do that again. Once I did that I felt so much better.

After that movie with my cousins I never watched a scary movie again, no matter how much my friends wanted me to. It just isn't worth it. There is no point. I enjoy living free from fear and anxiety too much to give them up for a couple hours of a thrill. The Bible tells us to guard our hearts.

Proverbs 4:23 (NLT) Guard your heart above all else, for it determines the course of your life.

You guard your heart by guarding your doors, your eyes, and ears. Heart in this verse means your soul, your mind, will and emotions remember we talked about that in an earlier chapter. Be alert to what you are letting into them. Be quick to shut any device off that is showing or playing something upsetting to your soul. It can be visual like movies or shows or audio such as music or a pod-cast. Be mindful of what you are hearing and seeing. None of it is worth leaving you open to be trapped by anxiety again.

There are many great shows, movies and music etc to choose from that won't bring in fear. Just use wisdom and listen to the Holy Spirit inside you.

> **Be mindful of what you are hearing and seeing.**

And if you make a mistake and realize in the middle of it that you shouldn't be watching this, turn it off or leave the room. This is one case where you don't have to finish what you started. You have the keys to your own doors. You use those keys wisely by making good choices. Choices made to impress your friends will never be worth it especially when you are gripped by anxiety and can't sleep and your friends are nowhere around. Real friends will want to do the same thing as you and guard their hearts too.

How to hear the Holy Spirit

The Holy Spirit leads us in every part of our lives. It is important that we know how to hear him, especially in the case of what we open our doors to and what we don't. For instance, there is a movie you would really love to watch. Your friends have all seen it and they say it's great. You haven't seen it yet and you certainly want to because you're not gonna be the only one who hasn't it, no way.

But when you are quiet, deep down inside you feel a hesitation, a feeling that maybe you shouldn't see it. You can't come up with a good reason why not but still that feeling is there. It's an uneasy feeling warning you not to go.

That is the Holy Spirit.

He speaks softly and he doesn't yell. To hear him you have to listen and pay attention. He will never say anything that goes against what God has written in his Word. God says stealing is wrong, the Holy Spirit will never tell you to steal, you see what I'm saying. The more you read the Word the more familiar you will be with the character of God and the easier it will be to hear the Holy Spirit. Also the more often you obey what he says to do the better you will hear him. If you get used to overriding that quiet voice inside with your own logic the harder it will be to hear him.

You want to hear and obey him because he knows the future, he's God. He knows why you should or shouldn't do something. It may make no sense to you right now at all but if he tells you to do it there's a very good reason you can count on it.

We've talked about how much God loves you. He only wants the very best for you. Sometimes our idea of what is the very best and his idea about it differ greatly. But as I said he knows what we don't. He knows what that movie, show, book etc is all about before you see it. He knows that maybe you'll have a few minutes of talking with your friends about how great it was for a short time and maybe for a minute you won't be the only one who didn't see it. But after everyone leaves and you are home alone in your room the fear that was reignited by opening your eye and ear doors to that thing will come alive in anxiety.

That anxiety that steals your sleep, your peace of mind, ability to focus and just enjoy life, is back. The friends aren't there but the anxiety is. Was it worth it? Was it worth not listening to the one who loves you most? No it wasn't. It never is, believe me, I know. So my point here is this, listen to and obey the Holy Spirit at all costs. Your life will be so much better than you can imagine. That momentary feeling of fitting in with friends will never compare to a lifetime of peace.

I encourage you to pray and ask God to help you hear the Holy Spirit when he speaks. Then when you hear, be quick to do what he says and don't open the doors of your heart to just anything.

Also this doesn't mean you can't see movies, or listen to music or read books or even play video games. God knows what you love to do because he made you. If you love music, he put that love in you. He isn't expecting you to just avoid music because it can potentially cause you anxiety. He will lead you to good uplifting music that you really like that makes you feel great when you hear it. The same thing goes for anything else like movies, books, video games etc. There are very good things on this earth to entertain you that will not hurt you at all.

We do not have to give up having fun. God is the designer of fun. He even laughs. He wants you to have fun because it's good for your soul. Just let him lead you to the best ways to have fun that will actually feed your soul and make you feel good, not leave you feeling scared and anxious.

Friend or Foe

Friend

To have fun, honest, good friends is the best thing ever. It's so wonderful to have people who share your interests and love what you love and laugh at the same stupid things you do. Good friends are a gift from God. He wants us to have them. He's the one who came up with the idea of friends. They should have a special place in your heart.

If you don't have any friends that believe in the Lord like you do, ask God for some. He wants you to have friends that are like you that can encourage you in your life with the Lord and whom you can encourage. If you have friends who try to lead you to do things you know you shouldn't do, those aren't friends you want to hang out with much. I know it's hard to walk away from friendships where you feel like you belong. But if they are not encouraging friendships that help you to be your best self, God has so much more than that for you. It may be hard to imagine, but he does.

Imagine a good life, a life of peace in your mind and confidence. Where you are loved by your creator, the one who knows you better than anyone.

He knows how much you long to be accepted by your friends. So trust him. If your current friends don't accept the new Christian you, God will give you new friends.

A good place to meet people and make friends that believe like you is church. If you don't go to church yet and are not sure which church to attend, pray about that. In other words, ask God. He will hear and lead you where to go. I recommend that you pray about everything. The Holy Spirit who lives inside you is there to lead and guide you. But he's a gentleman and doesn't push. When you ask him, he will help you know what to do and where to go. That's his job and he's good at it.

Here's an example of a way he might lead you. Say you hear someone talking about a great church and on the inside you'll just know you should try it out. You may see an advertisement for a church on Facebook or some other social media. The Holy Spirit leads gently and you could even think it's your own idea but it's him leading you. Make sure the church you go to teaches from the Bible and not someone's opinion or another book

.

The Bible is God speaking to us. We need to know what he says. Good pastors and teachers are gifted by God to help us understand the Bible and what God is saying. Within that church you attend, a good way to meet Christian friends is to join the youth group, Bible study, or young adults group.

These groups are great places to talk to people and get to know them as well as study the Bible.

God can and will often use Christian friends to help us know the right things to do. I've often been praying and asking God what to do about a certain situation, then soon a friend says something to me and I know that was my answer. God used my friend to speak to me. I'm so thankful for Christian friends. You will want some too.

If you have friends who are not Christians but don't pull you down and who really care about you and you care about them, then those are friends you should definitely keep. It's good to have those kinds of friendships because you can be a good influence on them. Don't be pushy about your faith. Let them know about your relationship with God but if they don't desire to ask Jesus into their heart, that's ok. Continue to be a good friend and example of what a Christian is like and pray for them. Someday they may change their mind and you'll be there to help them. But if they consistently try to pull you into doing things you shouldn't do, you may have to drop the friendship.

The lines of right and wrong are quite blurry these days, but the Bible is always the truth. So anything the Bible says not to do is something you shouldn't do, no matter what everyone else does or how you personally feel about it.

As a Christian, we are supposed to be learning what the Bible says and doing it. If you want to stay out of the anxiety trap then don't play games with truth. We already talked about not opening the door to the devil so there is no point going into that again.

FOE

We have mentioned the devil a number of times so let's talk about who he is and where he came from.

II Corinthians 2:11 (NLT) so that Satan will not outsmart us. For we are familiar with his evil schemes.

This verse does start in the middle of a sentence in every version I looked up but what matters is that it's clear that we are supposed to be aware and even familiar with the devils evil schemes. That means you can tell when he's up to no good and you can put a stop to it. It will help to have some background on who he is and why he is so bent on making us miserable.

Isaiah 12:-15 (NLT) "How you are fallen from heaven, O shining star, son of the morning! You have been thrown down to the earth, you who destroyed the nations of the world. For you said to yourself, 'I will ascend to heaven and set my throne above God's stars. I will preside on the mountain of the gods far away in the north. I will climb to the highest heavens and be like the Most High. 'Instead, you will be brought down to the place of the dead, down to its lowest depths.

Ezekiel 28:b-17 (NLT) "You were the model of perfection, full of wisdom and exquisite in beauty. You were in Eden, the garden of God. Your clothing was adorned with every precious stone—red carnelian, pale-green peridot, white moonstone, blue-green beryl, onyx, green jasper, blue lapis lazuli, turquoise, and emerald—all beautifully crafted for you and set in the finest gold. They were given to you on the day you were created. I ordained and anointed you as the mighty angelic guardian. You had access to the holy mountain of God and walked among the stones of fire. "You were blameless in all you did from the day you were created until the day evil was found in you. Your rich commerce led you to violence, and you sinned. So I banished you in disgrace from the mountain of God. I expelled you, O mighty guardian, from your place among the stones of fire. Your heart was filled with pride because of all your beauty. Your wisdom was corrupted by your love of splendor. So I threw you to the ground and exposed you to the curious gaze of kings.

These scriptures are talking about the devil/Satan. He was created a guardian angel, beautiful and full of wisdom. He served God. But then he became full of himself and evil pride was found in him. He was jealous of God and thought he should be above God and that he was better than God. Can you imagine that?

God created everything including Satan himself and he thought he should be above God. He didn't want to serve God anymore. He wanted to be God. And God knew what was in his heart. So he was thrown out of heaven to the earth.

Luke 10:18 (NLT) "Yes," he told them, "I saw Satan fall from heaven like lightning!

The person speaking in this verse is Jesus and he saw Satan be kicked out of heaven. Since Satan now hated God the first thing he did, when God created people that he loved, was to deceive these people into disobeying what God said. And they fell for it. They disobeyed by eating fruit God said not to eat and they sinned. Sin separates us from God and that's what Satan wants. He still tries to get us to disobey God today because he wants us separated from God.

II Corinthians 11:14 (NLT) But I am not surprised! Even Satan disguises himself as an angel of light.

This verse means he will try to make bad things look good. He will use reasoning so you will not see why doing certain things could be wrong. After all, everyone else does it and it's not hurting anyone.

You'll want to remember this. If God said it's wrong, then it's wrong. End of story. God defined right and wrong for us because he loves us so much.

If God said it's wrong, then it's wrong. End of story

He knows what the consequences of our actions will be even when we don't see them.

I'm not going to give you a list of do's and don'ts here. But I'd advise you to read the Bible, especially the New Testament and get to know God. Read what Jesus did on earth and you will know what God is like. Then you will know what is right and what is wrong.

When you start to understand the character of God, it will be harder for Satan to deceive you. The Bible calls Satan a deceiver and a liar. He is incapable of telling the truth. Don't let him steal your peace of mind by giving you fear and anxiety. Those are both from Satan, and you don't have to take them.

I John 4:4 (NLT) But you belong to God, my dear children. You have already won a victory over those people, because the Spirit who lives in you is greater than the spirit who lives in the world.

You always have the ability to chase Satan away. When you do, he has to leave. You never have to listen to him telling you you'll always have an anxiety problem, or God doesn't love you or you've been too bad for God to forgive you. He is a liar. Don't believe his lies. You can live in peace knowing you are forgiven and loved by God and God wants that for you.

Owned by Your Phone

Let's talk about social media. I like social media myself. I have a few different Instagram, Facebook, and YouTube accounts for my art business and ministry and a personal one. But I try hard not to have my face in my phone all the time. I've realized that I miss what is going on around me and I don't want to do that. I don't want to miss the things happening around me that may never happen again. Also we send others a clear message when we are with them, but are on our phones instead of talking to them, that they are not as important as social media is to us. Let's face it, everyone does that these days. But it's still rude.

When we have the opportunity to actually socialize in the presence of real people who aren't on a screen, we need to take it. Being with people, as we discussed in a previous chapter, fills our souls. It is the food our souls need to function right. Sitting next to a person while we're both on our phones just isn't the same. To ignore real people to look at a screen is quite rude. It is a gift to be with people we care about, to talk and laugh and share life. We need to stop giving people in our lives no value because of a screen. Focusing on our phones instead of people will hurt us in the long run.

Then there is the ridiculous thought that what we see on social media is true. Some of it may be, but there are a lot of misconceptions. Most people only share the good things in their life. They share about the great party they went to, the super hair style they have, a selfie where they look so thin and beautiful etc... But what we don't see is that though they were invited to that party and we weren't, they felt so lonely and out of place when they were there, or how that hair style was great at the beauty shop but for the life of them they can't get it to look that way at home, or how that selfie took 20 times to get right and needed different filters to make it perfect.

What you can't see is that each one of these people has a really bad self image but wants you to think they don't. No one's life is perfect but we can make it look like it is on social media.

If you're not careful it's easy to start feeling jealous of the great lives other people seem to have. We look at our own lives and they are not nearly as great. But it's a lie! Their lives aren't perfect and ours aren't awful. Comparing your life to an Instagram or Tik Tok snippet of another person's life is ridiculous. It's not comparable. You have good days where your hair looks great and your clothes fit perfectly and you have a great day at school. But you also have bad days where the opposite is the case. And so does everyone else on the planet.

I can give you references to studies that have been done about how social media can affect you in a bad way but you probably won't read them and I don't blame you. I probably wouldn't either. But you are smart enough to know that sometimes after spending time online checking out what your friends or influencers are putting on their pages you feel kind of sad. This is also a place that can cause fear and anxiety to come on strong. That fear of not measuring up to other people is a tough one. We all feel that at some point but real anxiety can come from that if you think about it for too long.

And too much phone time is to blame. Satan can use things like this to steal your self worth and make you feel lower than low. Remember the Bible verse we've looked at earlier.

John 10:10 (NLT) The thief's purpose is to steal and kill and destroy. My purpose is to give them a rich and satisfying life.

Remember the one speaking in this verse is Jesus. The enemy is Satan. Jesus wants to give us a good life and the devil doesn't. He will use whatever means possible to steal (like steal our self image), kill (like kill our relationships with others) or destroy (like destroy our good future). Don't let that scare you.

You are stronger than him and you can stop him in his tracks. Change that kind of thinking and choose to believe instead what God says about you.

There is a list in the back of this book of confessions based on scripture. Read them out loud and let your own ears hear them. You'll be surprised how your feelings change when you hear the truth. The Bible is always true. It is not just a bunch of nice stories, opinions or fiction. It is the truth. And when you read it out loud, that truth will chase out the lies and peace will come into your heart.

I'm not saying social media is all terrible because I don't think it is. I surely wouldn't have any social media accounts if I thought it was all bad. I think it can be used in a great way. We can be entertained, learn some cool things and connect with people in a healthy manner. But it takes a mature person to know not to believe everything you see on social media, and also know when it's time to put your phone away.

Another way you can be owned by your phone is to text all the time. When you text someone, you can never tell the tone in their voice, and that can lead to miscommunication. You will need to send texts, but it's not smart to carry on a constant conversation through texting.

Use your phone for social media and texts and maybe even calls, but just don't let the phone own you. When your phone owns you, you will easily slip into the anxiety trap and you won't realize how you got there.

I try to keep my mind free from being constantly bombarded with useless information that just upsets me. Sometimes I realize I'm spending too much time watching useless videos or looking at silly posts. I have to practice putting the phone down and doing something else. I'm not gonna lie, it's not always easy. This crazy phone is addicting. But it's not worth how I feel after consuming so much junk by scrolling mindlessly. I don't want to fight those feelings of jealousy, anger, self pity and fear. All those feelings can lead to anxiety and I don't want any part of that again. I don't want to get stuck in that trap. Do you?

It is important to be led by the Holy Spirit. He will let you know when you've had enough time on your phone.

I don't want to get stuck in that trap. Do you?

You'll know by the uneasy feeling inside you that you are overdoing it. If you ignore that feeling it will be harder to know when he's leading you next time. So do yourself a favor and don't ignore it. He's here to help you so let him do that.

God knows what triggers fear and anxiety in you and so does Satan. If we don't obey God in this then we can't be surprised when we start feeling anxiety coming on inside our minds.

Satan will make sure you see and hear what will hurt you. He knows exactly how to upset you. So don't give him that kind of access by not obeying the Holy Spirit's leading on the inside. Obey as quickly as you can when you start to realize your phone is getting too much of your time, and you'll be walking in the opposite direction of the anxiety trap.

Think About What You Are Thinking About

What ya thinking about?

Have you ever been asked that before? It's a particularly good question to ask yourself. What is happening in your mind that no one knows about?

Most of us go about our days just doing what we do and thinking what we think and never really considering it. But our thoughts are very important. They control what we do and what we say.

The Bible says **Luke 6:45 (NLT) A good person produces good things from the treasury of a good heart, and an evil person produces evil things from the treasury of an evil heart. What you say flows from what is in your heart.**

The Bible wasn't written in English originally. The Old Testament was written in Hebrew and Aramaic and the New Testament was written in Greek. The word "heart" in this verse in the original Greek is the word Kardeeah. I have no idea how to say it but it means "thoughts or feelings (mind)." So this is saying what you constantly think will find its way out of your mouth. We talked about your thoughts and words briefly in an earlier chapter but we will be going into that a bit deeper here.

Let's talk first about the importance of your words. I'm quoting a few verses of the Bible here so we can read it then we will go over it verse by verse to make sure we understand it.

James 3:2-6 (NLT) Indeed, we all make many mistakes. For if we could control our tongues, we would be perfect and could also control ourselves in every other way.
We can make a large horse go wherever we want by means of a small bit in its mouth. And a small rudder makes a huge ship turn wherever the pilot chooses to go, even though the winds are strong. In the same way, the tongue is a small thing that makes grand speeches. But a tiny spark can set a great forest on fire. And among all the parts of the body, the tongue is a flame of fire. It is a whole world of wickedness, corrupting your entire body. It can set your whole life on fire, for it is set on fire by hell itself.

The first part of verse 2 says **Indeed, we all make many mistakes.** Well that's certainly true isn't it? None of us are perfect. We all make mistakes.

For if we could control our tongues, we would be perfect and could also control ourselves in every other way. Wow! That is something to think about. If we could control our mouths (the word tongue used here in these verses is referring to our mouths and the words we speak with them) we could completely control ourselves.

Well I don't know about you but that tells me I need to pay attention to what I have been saying!

Has your mouth been negative and hurtful to others? Have you spread gossip or rumors? Have you been disrespectful or mean to a teacher or your parents? There is a lot to think about here. Because if we control what comes out of our mouths we can control ourselves in every other way. That is very important to remember. If you have had a problem controlling your bad habits of smoking, drinking alcohol, lying etc, you will be better at controlling those things if you clean up your mouth.

Verse 3 **We can make a large horse go wherever we want by means of a small bit in its mouth. When you ride a horse.** There is a halter that goes on the horse's head and a metal bar called a bit that goes in the horse's mouth. The reins held by the rider are attached to each side of the bit. The horse is trained to move according to how the rider pulls on the reins which pull the bit in its mouth. The horse can tell which way the bit is being pulled and that tells it which way to go. If the rider pulls right on the reins the horse will go right. A small child can even move a great big horse by the small bit in its mouth.

Verse 4 **And a small rudder makes a huge ship turn wherever the pilot chooses to go, even though the winds are strong.**

Where I live in Michigan, we have the Great Lakes around three sides of our state. Shipping is a big industry on those lakes and there are some very long ships that sail up and down the lakes and rivers of the Great Lakes system. There are 13 ships on the Great Lakes that are more than 1000 feet long and there are tons of other smaller ships. Currently the longest ship on the lakes is the Paul R. Tregurtha. It is 1013 feet long and 105 feet wide. To give you an idea of how long that is, the Empire State building in New York City is 1250 feet tall. If you put the Paul R. Tregurtha on its end and stood it up to the Empire State building it would only be a little bit shorter.

These big ships can carry a lot of cargo and that cargo is often iron ore. One ship in one load can carry the same amount of iron ore as 2,800 semi trucks. Are you starting to understand how big these ships are? I have always loved watching the ships. They are so amazing to me. One of my most favorite things to do is watch a 1000-foot vessel make an extremely sharp turn. Some of the rivers that connect the Great Lakes twist and turn and those ships amazingly just sail right through. How do they do it? With a small rudder in the back. The rudder is a piece of metal behind the ship's propellers. When the captain turns the wheel, it turns the rudder and the whole ship turns. Compared to the size of the ship, the rudder is quite small. Yet without it the ship cannot turn. Even in strong winds the ship can be turned by using the rudder.

Verse 5 **In the same way, the tongue is a small thing that makes grand speeches. But a tiny spark can set a great forest on fire.** We can say whatever we want because we have the right to, but it is never wise to let that mouth run wild. A tiny spark can set a whole forest on fire. A badly placed word from our mouths can do the same thing. We can cause much destruction in our own lives and our relationships with others by our mouth.

Verse 6 **And among all the parts of the body, the tongue is a flame of fire. It is a whole world of wickedness, corrupting your entire body. It can set your whole life on fire, for it is set on fire by hell itself.** These are some strong statements. Controlling what we say is one of the most important things we can do. When we speak words that create fire like pain or torment, we are letting ourselves be a mouthpiece for the devil. That is a very hard thing to face. But we have all done it.

All these verses are showing us that something very small creates a very large action. Our mouths are very small compared to the rest of our bodies but they can change our lives and others lives for good or bad. We have a big responsibility to control our mouths. You might know people who think it's ok to say whatever you want to. Maybe you've even thought that you should say anything that comes to your mind.

But now you know that one word from your mouth can be the thing that creates a huge impact on someone else or in your own life. If you say something that hurts someone, you cannot take those words back. Once they are out of your mouth, they are out there. It's much better to control our mouths because then we can control other parts of our lives and that's worth it.

Since what we say comes from what we think then doesn't it make sense to think about what we are thinking about? Anxiety in your mind starts with what you are thinking about. You know those times you are just staring out the window but at the same time you're mulling something in your mind over and over.

Well, take a minute to think about what exactly is going through your mind. If it's anger, sadness or hopelessness it's from the devil. Anything like "I'm stupid" or "I'm ugly" or "Nobody really likes me or loves me" are lies. Don't believe any of that and definitely don't let that stuff fill your thoughts. Those lies are like poison in your brain. And the anger and lack of self worth caused by that kind of thinking can spill out of your mouth and set a fire you can't put out. Instead meditate on what God's word says. He loves you and has a great plan for your life.

Jeremiah 29:11 (AMP) For I know the plans and thoughts that I have for you,' says the Lord, 'plans for peace and well-being and not for disaster, to give you a future and a hope.

Here is an interesting thing in all of this. You can actually tell your brain what to think. You're actually the one in control here. And it's much easier to change thoughts by speaking out loud than it is to change thoughts by thinking. So am I telling you to talk to yourself? Why yes I am. I often have to quote scripture to myself out loud to make myself stop thinking things that aren't good for me. It isn't always easy, but boy is it worth it. And if you start this habit when you're young you will be so happy you did.

Your life will be much better (still not perfect) but much better if you control your mind and your mouth from a young age. Remember your mind and mouth work together and can help or hurt each other. So get your thoughts under control and let your mouth help. Then keep your mouth under control and let your mind help.

There are lots of wonderful promises that God has given us that you can choose to think about. I have a list in the back of this book of scriptures and confessions. Confessions are statements that are based on God's word. Maybe you've heard of positive affirmations, saying positive things about yourself out loud so you can hear them. Confessions are the same thing except they are absolute truth based on God's word. When the creator of the universe makes a promise to you it's a guarantee. Speaking what God says but changing the words to make it a personal truth is very powerful.

I'll give you an example. The Bible says in **2 Timothy 1:7 (NLT) For God has not given us a spirit of fear and timidity, but of power, love, and self-discipline.**

Now this is how you make that verse personal so you can speak it out loud to yourself: *God has not given me a spirit of fear or timidity, but he's given me power, love, and self-discipline.*

As you read the Bible or as you hear a sermon, sometimes you'll notice a verse you hear really speaks to you. Look it up, write it down, and make your own confession from it. That's not wrong. That's how you apply God's word to your own life and that will always be right.

Another way to fill your mind with truth is to memorize scripture. You know how to memorize facts and phrases for tests, so do it with God's word. It can be a fun way to challenge yourself and defeat anxiety in the process.

Anxiety comes from what we are constantly thinking about, so don't let your mind camp out in unhealthy places. Controlling your thoughts will benefit you and everyone around you. It's not good to let your mind go wherever it wants. It will go back to bad thinking if left unchecked. Pay attention to what is happening in your thoughts and think about what you're thinking about.

> Anxiety comes from what we are constantly thinking about.

Fighting the Good Fight

I don't much like the idea of fighting, but strangely the Bible tells us to fight the good fight.

I Timothy 6:12 (NKJV) Fight the good fight of faith, lay hold on eternal life, to which you were also called and have confessed the good confession in the presence of many witnesses.

This verse is telling us to fight because staying in faith can require a fight. It's easy to think you are believing what God said, but then you look back at the problem you have and you step right out of faith and into fear.

To understand this better, let's look at the definition of faith. Faith is defined by the Bible itself. We're going to look at it in two different versions of the Bible. Sometimes that can help us understand the verse better.

Hebrews 11:1 (NKJV) Now faith is the substance of things hoped for, the evidence of things not seen. And the same verse in the (TPT) **Now faith brings our hopes into reality and becomes the foundation needed to acquire the things we long for. It is all the evidence required to prove what is still unseen.**

Faith is what we truly believe. We talk about it as being in faith or out of faith and in this context we're talking about having faith in what God has said in his word, the Bible. That's being in faith. Out of faith means being in a state of fear and unbelief which is not believing what God has said.

Sometimes it's hard to tell what you truly believe and if you are actually in faith. Sometimes we think we believe what God has promised but we are actually worrying about our situation.

Faith is what we truly believe.

We would like to believe that what God said is true, but we just can't seem to stop being nervous inside.

I know this feeling all too well. I have had times in my life where I read the promise of God and tried so hard to believe it, but really I was just worrying about it and hoping that maybe the promise was true. This is where the fight of faith comes in. This is a pretty mature concept but if you learn it while you are young you will be so glad you did and you will actually be very spiritually mature for your age. This is one of those things however that you will have to relearn over and over through your life. Although it does get easier the more you do it. As you go through life you will have new experiences and challenges and the devil loves to find new ways to bug you. So you will need to rise up in faith again in each new challenge.

Why, you say, is faith so important? Because we receive everything God has promised us by faith. When you read in the Bible the books of Matthew, Mark, Luke and John (which are called the gospels) it tells us about Jesus' life when he was in human form on the earth. One of the things he did a lot was heal people. Often he told them their faith made them whole or healed. They believed what he said and they got what they believed.

Another reason faith is so important is found in **Hebrews 11:6 (NLT) And it is impossible to please God without faith. Anyone who wants to come to him must believe that God exists and that he rewards those who sincerely seek him.**

It's very clear here that God wants us to trust him and be in faith. He likes it when we just choose to believe what he says. But don't most people feel that way too? I personally love it if I tell someone that I'm going to do something and they believe me. And then on the other hand I really don't like it when I tell someone I'm going to do something and they don't believe me. I'm not perfect but I'm not a liar. I expect to be trusted, don't you? God is certainly not a liar either and he expects to be trusted also. And he's far more trustworthy than you or I!

Many people say everything happens for a reason, which is just another way of saying everything that happens is God's will and his plan.

While these people mean well, and that makes an inspirational Instagram post, it's not actually true. No where in the Bible does it say everything happens for a reason, or that everything that happens is God's will. If that were true, why would we even need faith?

Our faith in God and his Word is what changes things. If everything that happened was God's will, then we would have no business trying to change it. Look at **2 Peter 3:9 (NLT) The Lord isn't really being slow about his promise, as some people think. No, he is being patient for your sake. He does not want anyone to be destroyed, but wants everyone to repent.** Also **Matthew 18:14 (TPT) In the same way, it is not my heavenly Father's will that even one of these little ones should perish.**

These two verses make it very clear that God wants everyone saved. (Saved meaning making Jesus Lord of your life and living eternally. The word "perish" in these verses means to die without knowing Him which is definitely not good.) That is his will and plan. But is everyone saved? No they are not. We all have a free will. That means God has given us the right to choose to follow him and love him. God will not make anyone choose him. He does not want robots, he wants children who love him and follow him because they want to. So is his will always happening? No it's not. That is one example.

Now here are some verses that show you God's will for healing:

Isaiah 53:5 (NLT) But he was pierced for our rebellion, crushed for our sins. He was beaten so we could be whole. He was whipped so we could be healed.

1 Peter 2:24 (NLT) He personally carried our sins in his body on the cross so that we can be dead to sin and live for what is right. By his wounds you are healed.

Psalm 103:1-3 (NLT) Let all that I am praise the Lord; with my whole heart, I will praise his holy name. Let all that I am praise the Lord; may I never forget the good things he does for me. He forgives all my sins and heals all my diseases.

Each one of these verses promise that Jesus carried sickness on the cross for us so we could be healed. It was an exchange. He carried the punishment for our sin and he carried our sickness so we wouldn't have to be sick. But do people get sick? Yes they do. Is that what God wants? No it isn't. So I say all that to say we live in an imperfect world where there is sin and imperfect people who make bad choices. There's a devil trying to make bad things happen to us but God has made us some promises.

2 Peter 1:4 (NLT) And because of his glory and excellence, he has given us great and precious promises. These are the promises that enable you to share his divine nature and escape the world's corruption caused by human desires.

God's promises are all over the Bible and he wants us to believe them. This is where faith comes in.

Now back to how to know if you are really in faith and believing God. When you are truly believing God, you will feel peace and joy. No worrying and fretting, just peace. And fighting the good fight of faith just means to keep reading and/or listening to the word of God until you believe it deep down into your heart so much that you have peace.

When I'm dealing with something like an illness or fear in my own life, I have to talk out loud to myself and speak God's promises about that particular thing in order to get my own mind under control and stop worrying. (The confessions based on the Bible in the back of this book will help you with this when you read them out loud)

It can be hard sometimes because my mind can go all over the place with goofy and scary thoughts. Maybe you've experienced the same thing. But when I choose to think about how much God loves me and wants the best for me, it changes my thoughts.

It may take some time and lots of reminding myself and reading God's word, but if I keep doing it, the truth will sink in and peace will come. And that's when I know I'm in faith trusting God. That's the absolute best feeling!

And it's right about then that the devil will send a person with a very discouraging story to try to get me back out of peace. A friend will text me about someone who died from the same ailment I have or they ended up broke doing something I've done. This is how a fight works - the enemy fires back when he thinks you're not expecting it. But I still win and you will too!

That's when I must choose what I allow to stay in my mind. If it doesn't build up my hope, then I don't listen to it. The answer to my prayer depends on me being single mindedly focused on the Lord and his truth. NOT the devil and his lies. And the same goes for you and everyone else. It works the same for all of us.

And it's not long after I've stopped focusing on my problem, I've chosen not to dwell on the nasty stories the enemy sends, and I instead let peace be the boss of my thoughts when the answer comes! I have some wonderful testimonies/true stories of God doing amazing and miraculous things in my life because I trusted him. One of those testimonies is how he rescued me from a pit of anxiety.

God does not want anxiety in your life. It keeps you from being the person he wants you to be and it can cause your life to go in a direction God never planned it to go. Anxiety is a big problem right now in the world. It almost seems like everyone has an anxiety problem and you're not cool if you don't have issues with it.

But it's not cool.

It's a trap.

And you don't have to be stuck in that trap. Let's review the keys I've given you to escape the anxiety trap:

- Go to God and surrender your life to him. That's called getting saved.
- Read the Bible and do what it says
- Pray and be in faith because God said he will help you escape anxiety, and your faith will make it happen.
- When necessary, fight the good fight of faith to continue believing God and don't back down.

Also remember if you need medical help please get it. But trust God to help you by using a doctor, counselor and medicine if needed. Continue reading the Bible and trusting God. He wants you to be free from the anxiety trap. Go to him and trust him to get you free because he will and you will have the good life God has planned just for you.

Scriptures and Confessions

The scripture references are written here and a confession in bold type is listed right after the scripture. Feel free to come up with your own confessions based on these scriptures if you'd like.

1. II Timothy 1:7 (NKJV) - For God has not given us a spirit of fear, but of power and of love and of a sound mind.

    I do not allow the spirit of fear to fill my thoughts with lies. I have power, love and a peace filled mind.

2. Deuteronomy 31:6 (NIV) - Be strong and courageous. Do not be afraid or terrified because of them, for the Lord your God goes with you; he will never leave you nor forsake you."

    I am strong and courageous. I am not afraid or terrified for God is with me.

3. Psalm 34:4-5 (NLT) - I prayed to the Lord, and he answered me. He freed me from all my fears. Those who look to him for help will be radiant with joy; no shadow of shame will darken their faces.

    I pray to the Lord and he frees me from all fear and gives me joy with no shame.

4. Psalm 23:4a (NLT) - Even when I walk through the darkest valley, I will not be afraid, for you are close beside me.

When things look bad in my life I am not afraid because the Lord is with me.

5. Psalm 56:3-4 (NLT) - But when I am afraid, I will put my trust in you. I praise God for what he has promised. I trust in God, so why should I be afraid? What can mere mortals do to me?
(This verse is a confession of its own)

6. Psalm 27:1 (NLT) - The Lord is my light and my salvation—so why should I be afraid? The Lord is my fortress, protecting me from danger, so why should I tremble?

The Lord has saved me and protects me. I am not afraid.

7. Isaiah 41:13 (NIV) - For I am the Lord your God who takes hold of your right hand and says to you, Do not fear; I will help you.

The Lord has my hand and will not let go. I will not be afraid because he will help me.

8. Hebrews 13:6 (NLT) - So we can say with confidence, "The Lord is my helper, so I will have no fear. What can mere people do to me?"
(This verse is a confession of its own)

9. John 13:27 (NLT) - I am leaving you with a gift—peace of mind and heart. And the peace I give is a gift the world cannot give. So don't be troubled or afraid.

I have the peace of mind that Jesus gives me. I will not let myself be troubled or afraid.

10. Philippians 5:6-7 (NIV) - Do not be anxious about anything, but in every situation, by prayer and petition, with thanksgiving, present your requests to God. And the peace of God, which transcends all understanding, will guard your hearts and your minds in Christ Jesus.

I refuse to be anxious about anything. I pray and God gives me peace that doesn't even make sense but it makes me feel so much better.

These 10 verses and confessions are a start for you. Find verses in the Bible that really speak to your heart then write your own confessions and say them regularly. It will be amazing how much better you will feel, and how much better you get to know God in the process.

If you don't have a Bible they are very easy to get and can be found where books are sold. Look at the different versions see which one seems the easiest for you to understand. The King James, although an excellent version is written in old English. I wouldn't recommend it for you first Bible. But there are many other versions to choose from to have an actual Bible you can carry and write notes in or/and download a Bible app. The You Version app is a good one. Its great and has many versions of the Bible in it.

Salvation Prayer

Father God I come to you in Jesus name. I believe that Jesus died on the cross to take my place. I ask you to forgive me of my sins and I want Jesus to be the Lord of my life. I will live to do his will and let him lead me. Holy Spirit please come and live in my heart and I will listen and obey you. Thank you father for washing my sins away and making me clean. In Jesus name. Amen

I'm praying for you.
If you prayed this prayer for the first time I'd love to know. Please contact me at
You can find me at Dailylifeinchrist@gmail.com

You can also find me @
Facebook-Daily Life in Christ
Instagram-dailylifeinchrist
Youtube.com/dailylifeinchrist

www.ingramcontent.com/pod-product-compliance
Lightning Source LLC
Chambersburg PA
CBHW071534120626
46550CB00006B/2453